Design and Build a Rockery

Contents

Introduction

A well-made rock garden makes a superb focal point in the garden, and a plantsman's paradise. Badly made, it can be a positive eyesore.

The first cardinal rule in building a rock garden is to use natural rock, and to build it so that it looks as though it is a natural outcrop. *Never* use broken concrete or builder's rubble in place of rock. You will simply finish up with a heap of old rubble!

Sometimes the travelling gardener will make a point of returning from holiday with a few small pieces of rock to build up a rock garden of cosmopolitan materials —another mistake. There may be some nostalgic pleasure in viewing the pieces of rock and remembering happy times in Majorca, Benidorm or Brighton, but the result will never be more than a hotchpotch, lacking continuity and line. Ideally, to get a good idea of how a rock garden should look, go out and view one in the wild. Take a trip to one of the many rocky areas in the country, and see how nature does it.

The rock garden must also fit in with the locality and the remainder of the garden scheme. A heap of soil thrown down in the corner of a suburban garden, with a few rocks dumped on it, will always look unnatural and out of place. If your garden is not blessed with a natural slope, the rock garden must be landscaped into it gently and carefully so that the change from flat lawn to rocky outcrop is gradual and unobtrusive.

In many cases, even if you are an alpine enthusiast and are considering a rock garden as a setting for your favourite plants, you may find that your garden does not provide the right setting for a rock garden, but may be more suitable for a rock wall or scree garden.

Generally, a rock garden is best used as a natural setting for a collection of rock plants, and should be built with this in mind. The rock is built up into a series of separate beds for alpine and rockery plants. It may look a little hard at first, but, once some of the rock is hidden with plants tumbling over it, it will blend in with its background to make a really attractive feature.

A rock garden can be a main feature of the garden, incorporating pools and waterfalls. But, before embarking on such a project, it's worth some careful thought. They are not at all easy to build and are fraught with dangers. An over-opulent water feature in the wrong setting will be an eyesore, and will never give you a moment's peace. But, in the right setting and built well, a good water feature can be striking in its interest and beauty.

Planning

Rock gardens are difficult to plan on paper. All that can be designed before you begin to build is the general shape of the feature in relation to the remainder of the garden scheme, and its position.

Site

Try to face the rock garden either south or west. Most of the alpine plants you will be growing in it will relish a sunny position. Allow some room at the back of the rock, though, since there are several worthwhile varieties that prefer some shade.

A background of shrubs and, if possible, small trees will set off the rock and make it look more natural. Allow for this in new gardens and, in established situations, try to build the rock garden where there is an existing background. Remember that the aim must be to try to build something as near to nature as possible, so a background of wooden fencing or a brick wall will never look right.

Ideally, there should be some slope, so if the garden is flat, an artificial slope will have to be built. This is not a difficult matter with rock, as will be seen from the chapter on construction, (p 16), but care must be taken to ensure that the slope is integrated gently and naturally into its surroundings. You will almost certainly need some extra soil to build the slope. If you are removing topsoil from another part of the garden, perhaps when excavating to make a patio, it can be put to good use when making the rockery.

Note that I have specifically said 'topsoil'. Don't try to make use of the subsoil removed from deep excavations. Nearly all rock plants need a well-drained soil, and will not flourish if grown in a clay subsoil. When carting the soil to the site, don't put it in the exact place where you intend to build the rock garden, for you will only have to move it again. Place it a little way from the site, where it is easily accessible.

Most rockery plants will do best where they are protected from strong winds. Wind has a considerable drying effect and will in fact be more damaging than dry soil conditions. The rock garden should therefore be sited in a position where it will be protected by a planting of shrubs. In new gardens, this should be allowed for in the overall garden plan.

Trees, however, should be sited some way away from the rock. Most rock plants dislike too much shade, but worse still is the dripping of water from overhanging trees. This could quite easily kill off plants, and such wet conditions are bound to attract slugs and snails.

Rockery backed by trees and shrubs

Planning

Setting the Rock

The selection of site, position and surrounds of the rock garden are really as far as you can go in planning. The actual building of the feature is a purely creative exercise, and depends on the nature of the stone; therefore it must be designed as you go along. There are, however, some hard and fast rules that must be obeyed if the rock garden is to look natural.

If you have looked at rock in its natural habitat, you will have seen that rock faces are made by the erosion of soil by wind, rain and snow. Nature never picks up rocks and places them in position as we are trying to do. The essence, therefore, is to make the rocks look as though they have been in position for centuries, and have become exposed by erosion: no easy matter!

Once nature has exposed the face of the rock by eroding the soil, the rock face itself becomes eroded; the softer parts are gradually worn away, leaving a pattern of cracks and fissures. These are our clue to how the rock face looked in its natural setting.

On examination, it will be seen that the cracks and fissures in the rock follow a 'strata-line'. This is no coincidence. The rock was originally built up layer by layer, over millions of years, the harder layers often being cemented together by the hardened remains of millions of sea creatures. It is the lime in this cement that is removed by erosion to give the rock its attractive fissured face.

With some of the softer sandstones, the fissuring is not apparent since the whole stone has been uniformly weathered. Even with this type of stone, however, much the same building rules apply.

Most of the strata lines in the face of the rock run horizontally when it is in its natural setting. There will also be some lines at right angles to these, that have been caused by cracking. To achieve a natural effect, it is important to ensure, when setting the rock, that the strata lines remain horizontal. Never tilt the rock so that the lines run at indiscriminate angles to each other and, unless you are building a completely artificial rock feature (see p 18), never stand the rocks on end.

It will also be seen that in their natural setting, individual rocks have a slight backward tilt into the side of the slope. This tilt should be reproduced in the rock garden.

It will be hard for the rock-garden enthusiast to accept that he will have to bury a large proportion of the rock that he has bought. But, particularly with the larger pieces, this is the only way to achieve the natural look. Small pieces can be set fairly near the surface, but the larger chunks *must* have about three-quarters of their bulk buried.

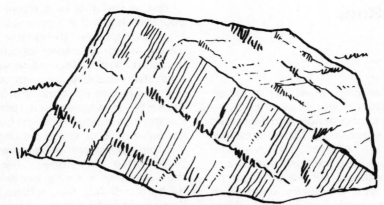

Rock showing horizontal strata lines

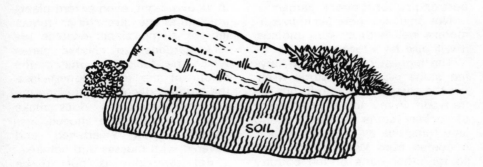

SOIL

Rocks should be well buried

Method of levering rocks into position

The Rock

There are many areas in the British Isles where stone occurs as a natural phenomenon and has been used extensively for building. There are villages all over the country where brick is unusual and stone cottages are the order of the day. If you are lucky enough to live in such a locality, then obviously the local stone is the best choice for the rock garden.

Not only is it more likely to harmonize well with its surroundings, it will also be a lot cheaper.

The biggest cost by far in buying stone is not the stone itself, nor the cost of quarrying it, but the transport. In my opinion, the *doyen* of rockery stone is Westmorland limestone, but, as its name implies, it comes from Westmorland, and so for other parts of the country the transport costs are enormous. Add to that the fact that, if you buy from a garden centre, the stone has to be off-loaded and then loaded and delivered again, and you can see why it costs so much.

But, if you live in a stone area, you will have the opportunity of buying direct from the quarry, thus saving a considerable amount in transport and handling charges, and also enabling you to select just the pieces of stone you need. Those of us who are not that fortunate can obtain stones from a garden centre or stone merchant.

Alpine-plant enthusiasts tend to prefer grey limestones, because they feel that it looks better as a background for the foliage and flowers of rock plants. Frankly, I feel that the rock must be beautiful in its own right, even before planting, and in any case, the great variety of alpine plants enables the rock gardener to choose plants which he feels will match the colour of the rock. Nonetheless, the craggy, deeply fissured nature of most limestones does make them very attractive indeed, especially when weathered and covered with mosses and lichens.

But sandstone is not to be sneered at, especially when it matches its locality well.

Weathered sandstone

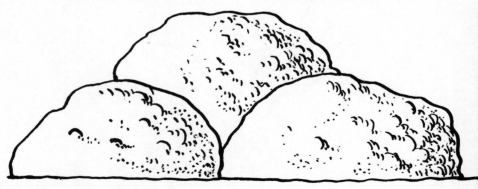

Sandstones vary in colour from almost pure white, through yellow, to browns and reds. Some are very soft and tend to weather quickly, but the harder types will last for many hundreds of years, with no more than a pitting of the surface. When weathered, they take on a beautiful, mellow appearance.

There are many other types of rock that can be used in the garden according to the taste and skill of the gardener. Granite, ragstone, marble, ironstone and even flint have been used to make very attractive rock gardens, but limestone and sandstone are undoubtedly the most popular and therefore the easiest to obtain.

Perhaps the odd man out is tufa. This is an extremely light, porous limestone which can easily be cut or hollowed out to take plants. It is expensive, but valuable for use in small gardens where a large rock garden would be impracticable.

Tufa can be hollowed out
for plants

The Rock

Ordering Stone

The great limiting factor when building a rock garden is the weight of the stone. Unless you have access to special lifting machinery, you must choose stone no heavier than you can handle. This will generally mean that the largest stones will weigh something like 150kg (3cwt). Rocks of this size will necessitate some help in setting them, and you will need strong boards and a few rollers (round fencing posts are ideal), to move them into position. A rock of that weight is no bigger than, say, the body of a garden wheelbarrow, so you will not get a great many rocks in a ton.

When ordering the stone, it is best if you can actually pick the pieces you want. If you are ordering from a distance, however, this is obviously impossible. In this case, let the stone merchant know exactly what you want. Tell him how many pieces weighing about 150kg (3cwt) you require, how many at 50kg (1cwt), etc. It is also wise to include a few 'chats'—small pieces of rock that come in very useful for wedging other stones into position. You will also find that they can be set closely together so that when the spaces between them are planted they look like one piece of rock.

A typical order for a small rock garden might be: 5 pieces at 150kg (3cwt), 12 pieces at 50–100kg (1–2cwt), 20 pieces at 50kg (1cwt), and 100kg (2cwt) of chats. This totals about 2.5 tonnes (2½ tons). It should be emphasized that this will make only a fairly small rock garden. So it will be seen that building a rock garden is a relatively expensive project.

Make sure that you will be at home when the stone arrives. If you are not, it is likely that the stone will just be tipped off the lorry. This will not only damage the rock, but it will probably do no end of harm to the driveway or grass on which it is tipped. It is far better, if the lorry driver is co-operative, to slide the rock off the lorry on boards. Some lorries are actually equipped with a small crane that will lift the rock off easily and without damage. If the face of the rock is damaged, it will stand out amongst the more weathered faces, and will take many years to weather down to match.

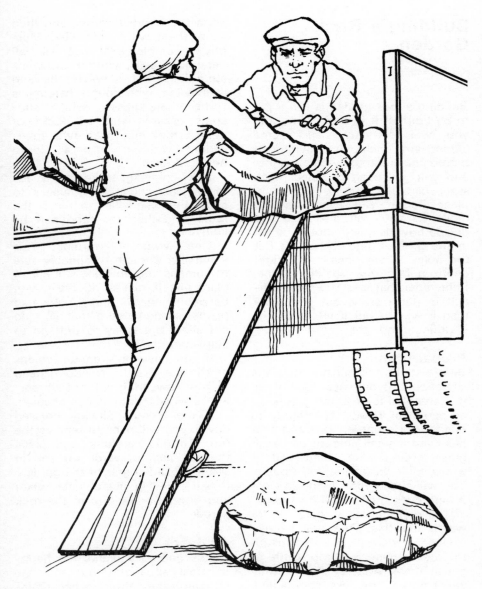

Using boards to slide rocks off lorry

Building a Rock Garden

Building a rock garden is not a job to be hurried. It is hard work, and you will certainly need some 'strong-arm' help. As mentioned before, it is an entirely creative job, and you will need to select each stone carefully and visualize it in place before you even start to move it. You will also need to decide how deeply it should be set in the ground, and try to dig out the holes to very nearly the right depth before you set the stone. Remember that it is far more difficult to get a stone out of a hole than it was to put it in—and that is difficult enough!

Preparation
Before starting to set the rock, the site should be prepared. First of all, it is essential to clear the ground of all perennial weeds. To attempt to build a rock garden on land that has even a small amount of couch grass, ground elder, bindweed or oxalis in it, is asking for trouble. You will spend years trying to clear it, and even then it will beat you.

The rock garden is paradise for weeds like this. They will happily establish themselves underneath the rocks where it is impossible to get at them. And, of course, they will smother the less competitive rock plants. The only thing to do in that situation is to remove all the plants and start again: not a happy thought. It is much better to start off properly.

To clear the ground thoroughly, allow the weeds to grow, and then spray them with weedkiller. Murphy's Tumbleweed will kill all perennial weeds, without contaminating the soil. If, however, the land is infested with tough perennials (other than grasses which succumb easily), such as docks or nettles, they may need two applications with at least a month between each.

After spraying, leave the weeds for at least a couple of weeks to allow the weedkiller to reach the roots, and then the land can be cultivated.

One word of warning. This weedkiller, though reasonably safe to humans and animals, will kill *all* plant life. It makes no distinction between wild and cultivated plants, so make sure that you do not allow the spray to drift on to cultivated plants.

If you have only annual weeds on the site, use ICI Weedol instead of Tumbleweed. It will not kill perennial weeds, but is much cheaper.

If the area is already grassed down, you will need to remove the turf. Do this carefully, and place the turf face upwards on soil in some unused corner of the garden. It will come in useful later when you slope the lawn up to the rock garden.

Drainage
Alpine and rock plants are happy in most situations, but the one condition they abhor is bad drainage. True alpines live in very rocky situations where drainage is always very good. True, you may also wish to grow a few moisture-loving plants, but these can be catered for specifically later on.

Remove turf carefully

If the land is heavy, or badly drained, it is well worth while digging off the topsoil and incorporating some drainage materials. Digging off the topsoil to the level of the firmer subsoil will also help to ensure that the rock is firmly bedded and will not sink. Be careful, when digging out, not to disturb the subsoil. If you dig too deeply and have to replace subsoil, some sinkage may still occur.

Dig out roughly the area that will be used for rock, and fill in the hole with drainage material. Crushed clinker or coarse ashes are ideal. If this is unobtainable, use gravel.

Moving the Rock

The first job is to move the pieces of rock to a position fairly near the site, and to space them out so that the faces and shapes can be easily seen. Always wear gloves when moving rocks; it is also wise to wear strong leather boots. The sharp edges of rocks can easily cut into your hands, and I need not say too much about the danger of dropping 150kg (3cwt) of rock on one's toes!

When moving the rock across established lawns, great care must be taken not to damage the grass. Most pieces will be possible to move with a sack barrow. These are the two-wheeled jobs like mini forklift trucks. The stone can be manoeuvred on to the platform and once the barrow is tipped and balanced, it will be quite easy to move. Sack barrows can generally be hired but make sure you get one with pneumatic tyres. They are much easier to push, and the tyres will not damage established grass.

Alternatively, you will need a few strong boards. Scaffold boards are ideal, and these too can be hired. Place a couple of boards on the grass and roll the stones over them. By moving the boards each time you reach the end, you can get away with using only four.

With very heavy or badly shaped stones, even rolling may be impossible. In this case, place some rollers underneath the boards and set the rock firmly on the boards. Tie a rope around the rock, and, with one person pulling and another pushing, it should not be too difficult to move even the largest rock.

Building a Rock Garden

Placing the Stone

With the rock set out around you, it will be easy to see which is the best face to show, and which part should be buried.

Start at the bottom of the rock garden and place the first stone near the middle. Get this one right for it will determine the line of all the others.

Decide first of all how much of the rock should be buried. To get the right effect, you should put at least half, and sometimes more, underground. It seems a shame to have to do it, but the finished result will be much more natural if you do. Dig out the hole to roughly the right size, shape and depth, and manoeuvre the stone to the edge of the hole. Now work it into such a position that, when it is finally rolled into the hole, it will be facing the right way. With the help of a good strong crowbar, it will be possible to move the stone a little afterwards.

Bear in mind that the stone should slope backwards by about ten degrees. If the slope is insufficient, lever up the front of the stone and wedge it with hardcore.

Now stand back and look along the stone to make quite sure that the strata lines on the face of the stone run parallel to the ground. Take your time over this crucial stage. Walk around the rock and make quite sure that the slope back into the ground is correct.

When you are satisfied that all is well, ram soil underneath the stone using a billet of wood. Do this really firmly, to make quite sure that no sinkage will occur.

If the stones are particularly big, and the soil is subject to some sinkage, it may be worthwhile building a few stones on to a bed of concrete. If further levelling is necessary, raise the stone and chock it up with hardcore as before, but this time, ram concrete underneath instead of soil. This should be necessary only with large rocks on soil that has been recently cultivated or has a high vegetable-matter content. Otherwise, normal procedures should be sufficient.

Use this first stone as the focal point of the first layer of rock, and build up other rocks in a rough horseshoe shape to provide planting areas.

Move large rocks with a sack barrow

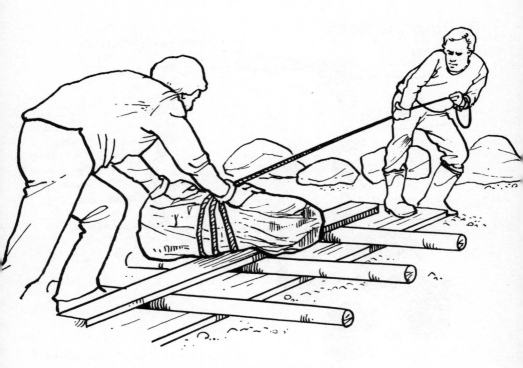

Method of moving large stones

Set rocks in a horseshoe shape

Building a Rock Garden

Cracks can be filled with plants

The greatest concentration of rocks should be in the middle of the rockery, thinning out a little towards the edges. This will help prevent the rock garden standing out like a heap of stones in an otherwise flat landscape.

When the first row is finished, build up a second row. Here the stone must be rolled either over the top of the first row, or from behind. Either way, you will need some good strong boards.

Try to achieve a balance so that the rock does not form itself into a conical mountain. The top level of the rock garden should be fairly flat, and never with an apex in the middle. Remember also, that a fair amount of maintenance will be necessary, so try to arrange the rocks so that they form a natural series of stepping stones for easy access.

Some gardeners suggest that the rocks should be filled in behind with compost. I prefer to fill in with ordinary soil, even though it may have to be dug out again later. It is difficult to decide at this stage which plants will go where, and this of course will determine the make-up of the compost.

Where two rocks butt together, fill in the crack between them by ramming soil in from behind. The crevice formed will make a good planting spot. Smallish stones can be built up by this method to look like one big rock. When the plants grow, the spaces between will be indiscernible.

Joining up

If the rocks have been skilfully positioned, they will slope gradually down to the lawn, with wider planting pockets nearer the edges. But if the lawn is flat, the rock garden will not merge completely with the rest of the garden layout.

There are two alternatives. First, the lawn can be gradually sloped up towards the rock garden to give the impression of a natural, gradual slope. To achieve this, you will have to cut the lawn back quite a way, depending on the size of the rock garden. Obviously, the bigger and higher it is, the greater should be the slope up towards it.

Start by cutting and carefully lifting the turf around the rock garden. Place the turf with the other that was lifted to make way for the rock. Now spread fresh soil and grade it to form a gentle slope. Bear in mind that the slope will be cut by a lawnmower, so it must be gentle. As the soil is added to form the slope it must be consolidated in layers.

Never spread more than about 15cm (6in) of soil without treading it well, with your weight on your heels.

When the slope has been graded to your satisfaction, the turf can be re-laid, tamping it down well with the back of a heavy rake. If you have been unable to lift the turf cleanly and evenly, it may be worth while buying in a fresh, machine-cut load. It will be much easier to lay level.

When the turf reaches the rocks, bear in mind that you will have to mow close to the edges so the turf should not finish too close to the rocks, where it will be impossible to use the mower. It is essential to make mowing easy and convenient, otherwise those edges will be left to look untidy, and that will detract from the overall effect.

At odd corners in the rock, where the mower will not reach, leave a planting pocket. At a later stage, you can set a few ground-cover plants to fill in. The second alternative is to leave a much wider space around the rocks and fill it with small stones.

If you are making a new garden, it is obviously best to build the rock garden before laying the lawn. Indeed, all the 'hard' landscaping should be done first.

Gradual slope to the rock garden

Rock Features

If your garden is very small and there is no room for a full-scale rock garden, or if it would be out of place in the garden scheme, you may wish to consider a rock feature. This is a much more formal arrangement of rocks and plants that make no pretence to look natural.

Many rock features owe a great deal to the influence of Japanese garden designers. In Japan the arrangement of stones is generally done to a quite rigid formula and often bears some religious or philosophical meaning. The Japanese have a different attitude to the design and use of their gardens, so their basic ideas need a certain amount of adaptation to suit the average European gardener.

The arrangement generally consists of three or four rocks of carefully selected shape. You will certainly need to visit the garden centre or stone merchant to select the rocks you need. They should be set in a formal pattern and in formal surroundings. An oval or circular bed cut in the lawn is ideal. They also make an excellent feature on the patio. Here, a

Formal rock feature

square, or better still a circular space, is left in the paving and filled with soil, and the stones are set to form a focal point.

When setting the stones, try not to be too fussy. The design should be intentionally stark and formal. A very effective arrangement consists of just three rocks—a tall one which is set upright, a flat one placed to one side and a little to the front, and another more or less round one, that goes between the two and, again, slightly to the front of the upright rock.

There is no need to bury the stones as deeply as you would if you were trying to make a rock garden look like a natural outcrop. You must, however, ensure that the tall upright stone is well bedded to prevent it falling over. If the stone is large, it will be safer to set it in concrete.

Plants for the rock feature need a lot of thought and careful selection. There will naturally be a temptation to overdo it. Resist it! The attraction of the feature depends mainly on the stone itself, so it would be a mistake to hide the shape of the rock by overplanting.

There are many small-growing plants that form a tiny, almost formal-looking cushion. These are ideal for planting around the base of the rocks.

If you have specially chosen your rock, there may also be a few cracks and crannies that can be planted with less demanding plants. Even these, though, should be treated with caution if they conceal the shape of the rocks or soften the rigidity of the lines.

Avoid tall-growing plants at all costs. The beauty of such a feature lies in the shape and balance of the rock, and this must not be upset.

Put plants between rocks and the edge of the grass

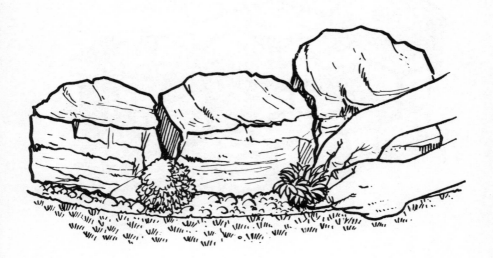

Dry-stone Walls

Another setting for a collection of rock garden plants can be provided in certain circumstances with a dry-stone wall. These are essentially informal features and will not look right in formal settings. They are fine in the cottage garden of a country house, epecially if the house is built with stone, but they would look out of place in the garden of a modern suburban house.

Walls with a single 'face' can be used to retain soil banks, or free-standing walls with two faces can be built. The building technique is slightly different in each case.

Retaining Walls
The dry-stone wall craftsman can build walls without a drop of mortar between them, and they will last for hundreds of years. A large part of the skill lies in selecting the right stones to fit together well. For our purposes though—to make a setting for rock and alpine plants—it is wise to bond the stones together with little soil. The selection of stones is still important, though.

Start by making a really solid foundation. Dig out a trench along the length of the wall, at least 30cm (1ft) deep and twice as wide as the wall. This can be filled with concrete, using a mix of 8:1 ballast and cement. Make the concrete as dry as you can work, since too much water weakens it. The top of the concrete should finish about 10cm (4in) below soil level so that it will not be seen.

Dry-stone wall

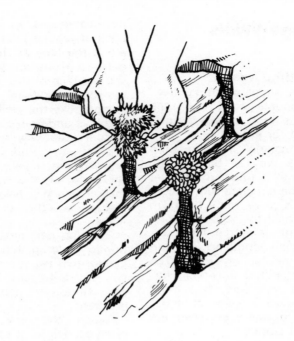

Planting as you build

When the concrete is dry, cover it with a layer of soil, and on this lay the first course of stone. Select the largest stones for these early courses, and as near the same thickness as you can find. Tap them down firmly into the soil, and tilt them just a little so that they slope very slightly backwards. The completed wall should lean backwards a little into the soil bank.

Fill in between the stones and the bank with more soil, and ram it down firmly. Now cover this course with soil and lay the next row, aiming as far as possible to make a bond, as you would when laying bricks.

When the wall has progressed to about 30cm (1ft) high, you can, if you wish, start planting as you go. It is much easier to do it this way than to try to work large roots into small holes afterwards.

The top of the wall can be left as it is, with trailing plants planted behind it, or a coping of stones on edge can be included.

This type of wall is suitable only if it is quite low, and provided the soil bank is not exerting a continual pressure on it. If the wall is high, or if the soil it retains slopes towards it, build a retaining wall of concrete blocks first. Don't forget to put weep-holes at intervals 30cm (1ft) from ground level, to allow water to drain out. Then build the ornamental wall in front of it. Alternatively, pack concrete between the wall and the soil bank.

Dry-stone Walls

Free-standing Walls

With a little bit of cheating, free-standing, double-faced dry-stone walls can be built to any height, and will last for ever.

Start by making the foundation in the same way as before. The higher the wall is to be, the deeper should be the concrete foundation. If the wall is to be more than 1m (3ft) high, or if the soil is subject to movement, reinforce the concrete with some lengths of old iron or special reinforcing rods. The wall is now built as previously described, but this time, two faces are built. Leave a space of about 30cm (1ft) or more between the two rows of stones.

When the wall is about 30cm (1ft) high, remove any soil that may have fallen down in the cavity, and carefully brush the backs of the stones to remove all traces of soil. The cavity is now filled with concrete, again using an 8:1 mix of ballast and cement. Tamp the concrete down well with a length of wood. The next 30cm (1ft) of wall can now be built up as before.

The great difficulty in building this type of wall is to get it straight. Because the stones are quite irregular, it is impossible to put a spirit-level on the face of the wall to ensure that it does not lean. There is a certain amount of leeway because the wall is meant to look uneven and informal, but if it leans too much it will offend the eye, and may even fall down.

The only way to check that it is not leaning is by looking. Step back at regular intervals, and look along the face of the wall. Try to get into a position where you can see the face of the wall in relation to something you know to be straight, like the wall of the house. If this is impossible, set a wooden post a little way away from the wall at each end, and level this with a spirit level. By comparing the face of the wall with this marker you will have a very good idea of whether or not the wall leans.

Planting can proceed as before during building, but you must be careful that the roots of any plants you set between the stones do not come into contact with the concrete.

When the wall reaches its required height, it can be finished off with a coping of stones set on edge. These are best set with cement mortar, using a 3:1 mix of soft sand and cement, since they will not be stable otherwise. Alternatively, leave the top 30cm (1ft) unfilled with concrete. This space can then be filled with a light compost and planted up. There will be sufficient drainage between the stones to allow excess water to get away.

(above) Check that the wall is not leaning

(below) Firm down concrete in wall cavity

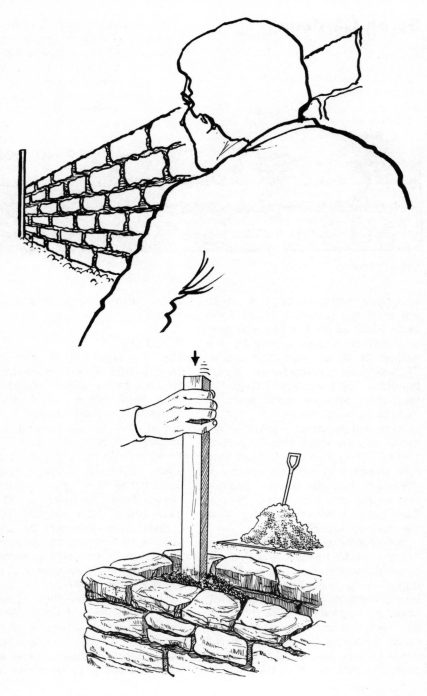

Scree Gardens

Scree garden

In nature, scree consists of steep areas of small stones. They have been crushed by a geological fault and further broken down by the action of wind, rain and snow. They provide a home for some very beautiful alpine plants that the enthusiast will certainly want to include in his collection.

Very often, scree gardens are made as part of the general rock garden. They can be formed into little plateaux in the rock garden or they can meander down between the rocks. As mentioned before, they can also form the link between rock and grass.

Alternatively, a separate scree garden can be formed, and this is a particularly useful way of making a home for a selection of alpines where there is not space for a full scale rock garden. Because relatively small stones are used in the construction of an artificial scree garden, they cannot be built on such an acute slope as they would

be in nature. So good drainage is essential.

Building

Start by providing a really well-drained bed. This is done by digging out to a depth of about 60cm (2ft) and filling with drainage material. Crushed clinker is ideal, but if this is not available, use builder's rubble or even gravel. There should be a depth of about 45cm (18in) of drainage material. On top of this, place some old turves face downwards. If you have made the garden on a grassed area, you will be able to use the turf you have stripped off. The layer of turf will prevent soil from washing down and choking the drainage system.

On top of the turf, spread a 15cm (6in) layer of scree compost. Two types of compost will be necessary if you are to grow a wide range of plants. Lime-lovers will need a chalky compost which can be made with limestone chippings, while acid-lovers will need to be grown separately in a lime-free mixture, using grit.

The compost should consist of three-quarters grit or stone chippings, and one quarter soil, leafmould or peat.

Scree gardens always look best if a few larger stones are set here and there to add a little height.

After planting the scree garden, cover the whole area with another layer of grit or stone chippings, so that it finishes right up to the crown of the plant.

Moraine Beds

Some more difficult alpines demand good drainage, but, when they are growing, they need constant moisture. These are the plants that, when growing wild, are watered by melting snow. The construction of a moraine bed is slightly different.

When excavating, make the hole slope slightly towards the centre. The bottom of the hole is then lined with concrete or a plastic pool-liner. Allow for drainage by making holes about 15cm (6in) from the bottom. Now fill with a 15cm (6in) layer of gravel and top up with scree compost.

The plants in this bed will generally receive sufficient water for good growth from natural rainfall, but they may need hand-watering in very dry weather.

Waterfalls and Pools

The incorporation of water in the rock garden will add a whole new dimension. The sight and sound of water trickling between and over rocks, the interest of a pond containing fish, and the increased scope for planting, add a wonderful variety of beauty and interest. But it is not a job to be undertaken lightly; unless it is done well, pools and waterfalls can be a source of endless troubles.

Planning

The waterfalls and pools must be planned from the start as an integral part of the rock garden. Never build the rockery first and then hope to incorporate a water feature at a later stage.

Check first of all on the size of pump you will need. This will depend upon the height to which you wish to raise the water and the amount of flow you require. It is possible to buy some quite large submersible pumps, and these are much easier to install since they do not need a special housing. They are simply dropped into the water.

You will also need an electricity supply, of course, and unless you are a competent electrician, it is better to get professional help to install it. Make sure that cables are sited well away from any area that will be cultivated, and that they are well buried in the ground.

The outlet of the waterfall should start somewhere near the top of the rock garden, and meander down it, changing direction from time to time. It should also empty into one or two smaller pools on its way down, until it finally reaches the largest pool at the bottom.

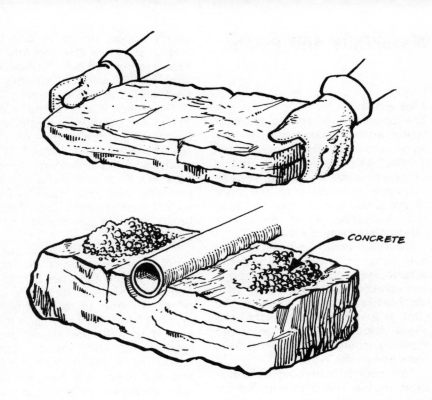

CONCRETE

Water pipe hidden between two rocks

Again, it is virtually impossible to plan the waterfall on paper. It will depend upon the rock that you have available. So start by setting out the rock where you can see it, and have some idea in your head as to the rough form the feature will take.

First of all, select the rock which will sit at the very top of the waterfall and set it on one side. Often you will have a few rocks with half-round grooves cut in them. These are made by drilling when the rock is quarried, and are ideal for carrying the water pipe.

Once the pipe is set, and a flat stone cemented over the top, it will be quite indiscernible. If you are not lucky enough to have one of these, choose a rock with a convenient depression in it.

The most useful rocks for the watercourse are craggy, flattish ones about 30–45cm (1–1$\frac{1}{2}$ft) thick. You will also need several flat rocks and quite a few chats. Bear this in mind when ordering.

Before you start work, have enough water pipe handy to run from top to bottom of the water-fall. Generally, a 13mm ($\frac{1}{2}$in) diameter alkathene pipe will be large enough, but for really big features, you may need 20mm ($\frac{3}{4}$in).

Waterfalls and Pools

The Pool

The bottom pool should be built first. Start by marking out the area to be excavated. This should be an informal shape, and can be marked either with pegs and string, or with a garden hose bent to the right shape. If you are building the pool with concrete, allow for 10cm (4in) of concrete all round.

Once the area has been marked out, bang in pegs all round the outside, and with a straight-edge and spirit level, align them all with the final level of the edge of the pool. It is most important that the edges should be level to avoid showing a large expanse of concrete above the water.

The pool should now be excavated inside the area marked by the pegs. Small pools need only be 45cm (18in) deep but larger ones will be better 60cm (2ft) deep. It is never necessary to exceed 90cm (3ft). For easy emptying, make the bottom of the pool slope towards one deep spot, and make the sides slope gently. If you intend to grow aquatic plants near the edges of the pool, build in some shelves about 23cm (9in) from the top of the pool. If you are building the pool with concrete, use a 6:1 mix of ballast and cement, and mix with the water the required amount of a proprietary water-proofing liquid. Starting from the bottom, the concrete is worked up the sides of the pool using a plasterer's wooden float. Try to ensure that about 10cm (4in) of concrete evenly covers the sides and bottom. Just before the concrete sets hard, mark a number of criss-cross lines on the surface, so that the final rendering will key into it.

The rendering is made with a 3:1 mix of sharp sand and cement. Don't make it too sloppy, or it will not hold to the sides. When rendering, it is important that the concrete floor and walls are kept perfectly clean and free from soil, so it is best to work from a strong board placed across the top of the pool.

Pools made with a plastic or butyl liner are easier to build. Simply stretch the liner across the hole and weight it down with bricks or pieces of stone. It is then simply filled with water, and it will stretch to take the shape of the excavation. The excess plastic round the edges is then cut off, and the edges are held in place with a covering of turf or stone.

Waterfalls are of such a permanent nature, and so difficult to repair, that my own feeling is that it is better to work in concrete rather than with liners. It must be admitted, however, that liners are cheaper and much easier to install than concrete. If you do decide to use a liner, reject the cheap polythene types; choose either reinforced PVC or, better still, butyl-rubber.

Concreting the pool

Position of rocks to channel waterfall

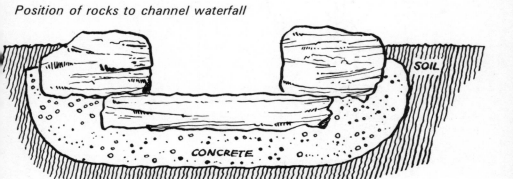

SOIL

CONCRETE

Waterfalls and Pools

The Waterfall

It would be foolish to suggest that building a waterfall is an easy job for the amateur gardener.

Ideally, the job should be completed in one day. This way, the concrete will have no chance to set solid between the laying of each stone, and will therefore bond to form a continuous channel. This is important, since bonding to hardened concrete or to stone is fraught with the danger of leakage.

It is also important to ensure that the soil underneath the concrete is well consolidated, since any sinkage at all could lead to cracking and therefore to leakage.

Start by digging out and installing the clinker or gravel drainage system as described for rock gardens.

Select a large, flat stone to sit on the edge of the bottom pool. It should be set in concrete made with a 6:1 mix of ballast and cement, with a waterproofing agent added to the water. There are several proprietary waterproofing solutions, available from any builder's merchant.

Set the stones on at least 15cm (6in) of concrete. When the bottom stone is firmly bedded, check that it is as level as possible. Ideally, the water should fall in a wide spread over the edges of the rocks rather than in a narrow channel.

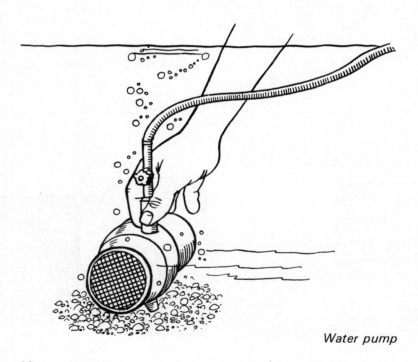

Water pump

The second stone is set so that it overlaps the back of the first. When this stone is set, place other rocks at the sides to contain the water. The concrete should be brought up behind these rocks to above the level the water will reach.

As building upwards progresses, change the direction of flow so that the water will zig-zag down the waterfall rather than run in a straight line.

It is a good idea to install one or two small pools in the course of the waterfall. These are made in exactly the same way as the large pool.

Installing the Pump

Unless the waterfall and pool are very large, a submersible pump will suffice. They are easy and cheap to install. A length of alkathene pipe is run from the pool to the top of the waterfall. It is best to take it over the side of the pool, rather than to build it into the concrete, since this would be a danger point for leaks. The pipe can be easily hidden by a covering of flat rocks.

Bury the pipe in the soil, and run it up to the top of the waterfall. If you have been able to select a rock with a convenient crack or a drill hole, it is easy to conceal it at the outlet. If not, cement a few smaller stones over it to hide it.

The electricity supply should now be connected up.

After building the waterfall, the remainder of the rock garden is built as previously described.

One small point: most submersible pumps come complete with one outlet for a waterfall, and one for a fountain. Resist the temptation to use both; mixing of the formal and the informal can never work.

Preparing for Planting

Once the rock garden is built, the planting pockets should be prepared. In some cases this will necessitate digging out the existing soil and replacing it with special compost to suit the needs of particular plants.

Before you even start, it will be necessary to get to know the needs of the plants you wish to use. Some plants prefer a chalky soil, while others like acid conditions. Within those groups are those that thrive in full sun, those that prefer shade, and others that will do best in very moist conditions. All these factors will affect the type of soil in the planting pockets and their position on the rock garden.

Most rock plants and true alpines prefer a soil that is not too rich in nutrients. Very fertile soil will simply produce very leafy plants at the expense of flower. The lush growth will also be likely to succumb to a hard winter and will be most attractive to the alpine's arch-enemies, slugs and snails. In nature, these plants grow mainly in poor, rocky soil, and it is these conditions that should be reproduced in the rock garden.

Mix soil with builder's rubble

The majority of common rock plants, however, will thrive on ordinary garden soil. Provided it is well drained, there is no need to do anything to it. If it is on the heavy side, mix a little coarse grit with it to lighten it. But, for the lime-haters, make sure you use washed horticultural grit—most other grits contain lime.

If you wish to grow lime-lovers, the best thing to mix with the soil is builder's rubble. There must be few places these days where it is not possible to find a house in process of being demolished. A little of the old, hardened mortar from between the bricks (there will be heaps of it lying about for the taking, though it's wise to ask first) will be ideal. If this is impossible to obtain, add garden lime to the soil.

Where acid-lovers are to be grown, the soil should be mixed with washed grit to provide drainage, and sphagnum peat to make the soil acid. Pockets for acid-lovers should be situated, wherever possible, above rather than below those for the lime-lovers.

If they are sited below pockets filled with limy soil, it is likely that rain water will wash free lime into the acid compost. Remember too, that, if it is necessary to water these pockets, it should be done with rain water. The free lime in most tap water will quickly turn an acid soil into an alkaline one.

When filling the planting pockets, make sure that they are filled a little above the level of the surrounding rocks, to allow for sinkage, and see that the soil is firmed a little.

Planting

Because rock plants are invariably pot-grown, they can be planted at any time. It is essential, however, to avoid planting when the soil is frozen or very wet.

Before planting, or even before ordering your plants, get to know something about their habit and the sort of conditions they like. Many conifers, for example, are catalogued as 'dwarf', even though they will eventually grow to heights exceeding 1½m (5ft). They would be more accurately catalogued as 'slow-growing'. Plants of that size would eventually dominate all but the very biggest rock gardens and look quite out of place.

Also, there is no point in trying to grow shade-lovers in a very sunny spot, or vice versa. They will never come to anything.

Start by selecting and planting the few specimen plants that will provide a focal point. These are best planted first so that a good balance can be achieved. Then divide the collection of plants into shade-lovers and sun-lovers, lime-haters and lime-lovers. The rock garden can then be planted systematically, starting at the bottom and working upwards. When planting, take into account the eventual spread of the plants. There is little point in overplanting. This will only result in the more vigorous species crowding out the weaker ones, and is a waste of money.

Unless you can beg your plants from a friend, all of them, even the larger shrubs and conifers, will be in pots. If you cannot plant them as soon as they arrive, put them in a sheltered part of the garden out of the full sun and water them regularly. Bear in mind that plants in pots are likely to dry out much faster than those planted in the open ground, so they will need a little personal attention from time to time. Give them a good final soaking immediately before planting. If the compost is well moistened, the young roots will suffer less damage when they are knocked out of the pots.

Set the plants out in their final positions before knocking them out of the pots. This will help you to achieve a better planting balance, and will save a lot of walking about too, when it comes to planting.

The plants should be held upside down and the pots gently tapped against a convenient stone or against the handle of the trowel. If the plants arrive in plastic bags, as many of the larger plants will, remove the bag by carefully cutting down the side with a sharp knife or a pair of scissors.

Make a hole with the trowel a little larger than the root ball and set the plant in it. It is important that planting should be at the same level that the plants were growing in the pots. Plant them too deeply and they will be subject to rotting. If they are too shallow, the top of the root ball will dry out and the plant may struggle to get away. Placing a short cane across the hole will quickly show you the correct level.

When the plant is at the correct height, sprinkle a little bone-meal

Firming in the plants

over the compost you have dug out, and refill around the roots. Firm the soil in with your fingers or with the handle of the trowel. Make sure when you firm, that you do not damage the root ball. The aim of firming is to ensure that the compost is in close contact with the roots all round, rather than to make the soil set like concrete.

After planting, give the plants a good watering, and remove all the debris of pots and plastic bags.

Then go round the rocks with a soft broom and sweep back any compost that may be covering them. Mulch round the plants, underneath the leaves and right up to the crown. For most alpines and rock plants, a fine shingle or coarse grit is the ideal mulching material. For some acid-lovers like heathers or dwarf rhododendrons and azaleas, a mulch of peat is preferred.

Cultivation

Perhaps the most important regular job in the rock garden is weeding. Until the plants are well established and spread to cover the ground, weeding may be something of an arduous task. This is why it is so important to start clean even before the rocks are set in position.

Hand weeding is really the only answer for annual weeds. To give the young alpines a good chance to grow without undue competition, hoe round them regularly. It will help if the mulch of gravel or peat around the plants is topped up from time to time, since this will help to reduce competition from weeds as well as to retain moisture and prevent evaporation.

If any perennial weeds appear in the rockery, they should be dealt with immediately. Once they get a hold, they will be extremely difficult to eradicate without disturbing the rocks. One good method of control is to treat them carefully with weedkiller. This can be done by painting the leaves of the weeds with weedkiller. Use a herbicide such as Murphy's Tumbleweed, applied with a paintbrush. This operation must, of course, be done with the utmost care, since the weedkiller is as deadly to cultivated plants as it is to weeds.

Paint leaves with weedkiller

In dry weather, watering may be necessary, though this must not be overdone. Alpine plants are more likely to suffer from rotting due to overwatering, than from drying out.

Strange though it may seem for alpine plants whose natural home

Couch grass

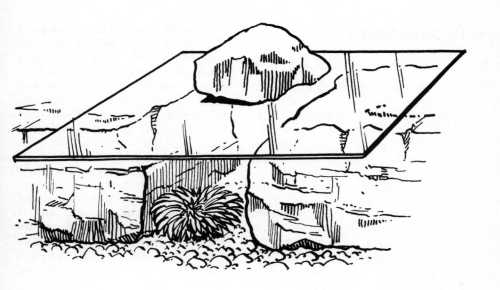

is the snow-bound mountains, many need protection during the winter. The reason is that, in their natural environment, they are covered in a warm, insulating layer of snow. Where this layer is absent, as it often is at lower levels, they can suffer from frost damage.

In warm areas, sufficient cover can be provided with a light covering of twigs or bracken. In more northern situations, however, some plants may need protection with glass.

The covering itself, though, is fraught with dangers, and should not be done until the first hard frost. Not only will mice relish the covering to make a snug winter home, with obviously damaging effect on the plants, but, far worse, the covering will restrict the free passage of air. This may result in attacks from fungus diseases, and subsequent rotting. Inspect plants

Protect rock plants with glass

regularly to ensure that they are not suffering underneath their covering.

In the spring, when the weather has taken a turn for the better, the covering should be removed. Keep it handy, though, in case it turns cold again.

After uncovering, check all the plants to ensure that they have not been lifted by frost, and re-firm them if necessary. Then hoe round them to aerate the soil, clean up any dead foliage, and cut off dead stems, ready for the surge of growth in the early spring. It may also be necessary at this time to replace soil that has been washed away during the winter, or to replace the mulching material.

Propagation

One of the easiest methods of increasing the stock of rockery plants is by seed. Most perennials and more common rock plants are best sown in a slightly heated greenhouse or frame in late winter or early spring.

Before placing inside, some seeds should be subjected to a period of freezing. This applies to many of the true alpines that naturally grow at high altitudes.

Use a compost consisting of a mixture of soil, peat and sand—John Innes seed compost with a little sharp sand added is ideal—or a soil-less mixture with sand, such as Arthur Bowers seed compost.

Sow the seeds in boxes or pans, and give the compost a good watering. Then cover them with glass and paper, or a piece of opaque polythene. This covering must be removed as soon as the first seedlings appear. Then place the containers in a light situation near the glass to prevent them from becoming leggy.

As soon as they are large enough to handle, they should be transplanted into pots or boxes, and subsequently moved on to individual pots. When they are growing well, they can be given more ventilation and gradually 'hardened off' before planting outside.

Transplant seedlings into individual pots

Rock plants that are readily and easily propagated by seed include: *Aster alpinus*, *A. subcoeruleus*, and *A. amellus*, *Aquilegia*, *Dianthus*, *Anemone*, *Bergenia*, *Erinus*, *Linum*, *Geum*, *Primula*, *Viola*, *Erigeron*, *Papaver*, *Saponaria*, *Corydalis*, *Mimulus*, *Lavandula* and *Tradescantia*.

Another popular and easy method of propagation is by division. This is done simply by lifting the plants and dividing the roots. It has the added advantage of revitalizing plants that have become old and tired. If the plant is old, remove only the outer, younger offsets and replant in fresh soil. They will grow with renewed vigour, and a greater profusion of flowers. Division can be done in the spring or early autumn, though in the latter case, they must be replanted in time for them to become well established before the onset of the cold winter weather. Plants that respond well to division are: *Primula*, *Phlox*, *Sedum*, *Gentiana acaulis*, *Saxifraga* and *Aster dumosus*, as well as most ornamental grasses.

Some other plants can be increased by detaching and planting runners or rhizomes. These are planted direct into the rockery and include: *Iris*, *Viola odorata*, *Cerastium*, *Phlox subulata*, *Anemone silvestris* and *Vinca minor*.

Many rock plants can also be propagated by cuttings. Detach short, non-flowering shoots, trim them just below a leaf joint and set them around the edge of a pot of sandy compost. Rooting will be hastened if the base of the cuttings is dipped in hormone rooting powder, and the pots are covered

Trim cuttings

with a polythene bag supported by a couple of canes. The cuttings can be taken at any time during the growing season. Suitable plants to propagate by cuttings include: *Thymus*, *Sedum*, *Phlox subulata*, *Iberis*, *Erica*, *Arabis* and *Helianthemum*.

Some plants can also be layered. All that is involved here is the insertion of branches into the soil. They should be pegged down with wire staples until they are rooted, when they can be detached from the parent plant and re-planted. Suitable species include: *Thymus*, *Dianthus*, *Vinca minor*, *Erica* and several *Daphnes*.

Alpines

There are hundreds of varieties of alpine plants and these will form the basis of the rock garden population. A collection of alpines will fascinate the plantsman, though it is probably better to make a start with the more popular varieties since these will prove easier to grow.

Aubretia deltoidea

Ajuga Useful ground-cover plants, most of the ajugas are evergreen and grow happily in sun or shade. There is a great variation in foliage and flower colours to provide an all-year-round show.

Alyssum The brilliant yellows of *A. saxatile* and its varieties make it a must for the rock garden. It goes particularly well with *Aubretia*, both flowering in the spring. They prefer a well-drained soil and a sunny position, and should be lightly trimmed back after flowering.

Arabis A common garden plant giving masses of white or pink flowers in spring.

Armeria The common thrift produces evergreen mounds of foliage and bright heads of rounded flowers. They are tolerant of most soils and conditions and are easy to grow.

Aubretia This is probably the most common of rock garden plants and with good reason. They are easy to grow, tolerant of most soils and positions and unfailing in the production of masses of brilliant red, pink, purple and blue flowers.

Campanula Apart from the low-growing herbaceous varieties already mentioned, there are several true alpine campanulas which deserve a place. *C. portenschlagiana*, *C. poscharskyana*, 'Stella' and *C. carpatica* are among the best.

Dianthus alpinus

Dianthus The alpine pink, *D. deltoides,* is a popular and easy rock plant. It has deep green, prostrate growth and produces flowers of brilliant red and lighter pink shades.

Gentiana One of our most sought-after rock plants, but rather difficult to grow. *G. acaulis* is easiest perhaps, but, even so, is rather shy to flower. The most reliable is undoubtedly *G. septemfida*. The gentians flowering late summer to autumn sport large trumpets of blue flowers. They do best in sandy soil with plenty of peat added, since nearly all gentians are lime-haters.

Hypericum Large, saucer-shaped yellow flowers, borne in profusion, make this a valuable addition. *H. fragile* and *H. polyphyllum* are particularly suitable.

Iberis The perennial candytuft. *I. commutata* is fast-growing and vigorous, but showy if there is space. For the smaller rockery, *I.* 'Little Gem' is to be preferred. Both have white flowers and are easy and tolerant.

Leontopodium Commonly known as Edelweiss, this is a popular and interesting plant. It has silvery leaves and curiously shaped white flowers.

Phlox The alpine phloxes form dense mats and are unfailingly covered with flower in May and June. They come in a variety of shades of red, pink, blue and white.

Phlox will retain their compact shape better if trimmed back after flowering.

Phlox subulata

Primula Most primulas like a moist soil and partial shade. They are available in a variety of colours from violet through lavender, blue, red and pink to white.

Saponaria The species *S. ocymoides* is easy to grow and very showy. It has a trailing habit and a profusion of pink flowers from May to July.

Saxifraga An enormous group, far too large to describe in detail. There is a great variation in colour and form. Best and easiest are the kabschia types, the mossy saxifrages and the encrusted or aizoon forms; not forgetting, of course, the old favourite, London pride, *S. umbrosa*.

The first to flower are the kabschias. These need good drainage, but prefer a soil that will hold water in the summer and a position out of full sun. They make hummocks of foliage, either green or silvery, and there is a wide variety of flower colour and form.

41

Alpines

The mossy saxifrages flower in April and May. These form rosetted hummocks of evergreen foliage from which they produce sprays of flower, mostly pinks and whites, and a few varieties in red.

The encrusted or aizoon types flower in May and June, the sprays of variously coloured flowers coming from encrusted, quite hard rosettes of green or silver.

In October, there is one variety that should not be missed. *S. fortunei* 'Wada's Variety' has crimson foliage and masses of white flowers. It prefers a cool, shady, moist position.

Sedum Another large group with great variety of flower and form. Some of the best are *S. spathulifolium* which has a prostrate habit and sports starry yellow flowers; *S. murale* which has red foliage and pink flowers; *S. cauticola* with deep pink flowers; and *S. spurium,* which forms a dense, prostrate mass of crimson flowers.

Sempervivum Commonly known as houseleeks, this is yet another very large group. They will grow and thrive in the very poorest soil, as is shown by the number to be seen growing on old roofs with no visible means of sustenance. They are ideal for the novice plant collector.

S. arachnoideum These are fascinating in that their tiny rosettes are covered in a fine cobweb of hairs. Others have much larger rosettes of various colours ranging from bright green to deep red with many variegated forms in between. The flowers of these are not very showy, but they are worth growing for the foliage alone.

Thymus Most thymes have aromatic foliage when crushed, and will give a bright display of flowers. The genus includes some types that will grow upright, while others form ground-hugging mats.

Houseleeks

Bulbs

There are several dwarf bulbous plants that can be used to good effect in the rock garden, to give a bright display in early spring. They should be planted from August to October in well-drained soil that is not too rich in organic matter. Planting at the correct depth is important. A good rough guide is to plant them about three times as deep as the size of the bulb.

Alium The onion family includes some good ornamental species. *A. moly,* the yellow garlic, flowers in June, as does the carmine *A. ostrowskianum.*

Anemone These tuberous plants need a well-drained soil if they are to survive through the dormant period. *A. coronaria* is available in many shades, while the dark blue *A. apenina* and the various forms of *A. blanda* are particularly good rock garden subjects.

Chionodoxa The Glory of the Snow likes a little more moisture than most bulbs, and a slightly shaded situation. It flowers very profusely.

Crocus A large group, most members of which are suitable for the rock garden. The 'botanical' crocuses, some of which flower in the autumn and some in the spring, are particularly suitable for the rock garden.

Eranthis The golden flowers of the aconites will give a superb show from very early in the year. They will seed themselves and spread freely.

Iris The spring-flowering irises are delightful. Particularly suitable are the yellow-flowered *I. danfordiae* and *I. winowgradowii,* as well as the blue shades of *I. reticulata.* All flower in February or March, and will continue to flower even when covered in snow.

Narcissus There are many varieties of the dwarf daffodil that are suitable for the rockery. *N. bulbocodium,* the hoop-petticoat daffodil, and *N. nanus* are especially to be recommended.

Tulipa tarda

Tulipa The so-called 'botanical' tulips cannot be excluded. One of the earliest flowerers is *T. kaufmanniana,* the waterlily tulip, which is available in many colours. The varieties of *T. fosteriana* are especially striking, perhaps the best being 'Madame Lefeber', a bright red. *T. tarda* is one of the most rewarding species, bearing pretty yellow flowers in April/May.

Herbaceous plants

Many herbaceous plants are wrongly classified in nurseries and garden centres as alpines. It does not matter, of course, since there are several low-growing subjects that are ideal for the rock garden and are generally easier to grow.

Anaphalis These grey-leaved plants look especially good planted near to *Berberis thunbergii* and the red-berried *Cotoneasters*. They will grow well in most soils and bear whitish-yellow flowers in summer.

Aster There are several dwarf forms of the garden Michaelmas daisies that make excellent rock garden plants. *A. alpinus* bears single, daisy-like flowers of blue, lilac and white. All have attractive yellow centres. They flower in May/June. *A. sativus atro coeruleus* is a small, tufty plant with sprays of bright blue flowers, over a very long period.

Bergenia A really robust plant, it will grow in almost any soil and position. It has large, fleshy leaves of green or bronze, and white flowers.

Brunnera macrophylla A plant that prefers a slightly shady spot and cool soil. It bears dainty sprays of blue flowers in spring.

Campanula There are many varieties of the Bell flower, one of the choicest of rock plants and not to be missed. They flower at a time when the main spring show of

Bergenia cordifolia

alpines is over, and are obtainable in a range of blue shades and in white. Most are happy in sun or shade and they are not fussy as to soil.

Convallaria Lilies of the valley prefer a moist soil. They will provide a superb show of white, bell-shaped flowers each year, but they are inclined to spread and become rather invasive.

Dianthus Dwarf pinks are among the most important of the rockery plants, and there are very many varieties. Among the best are those that form tight cushions of flower ranging from light pink to deep red.

Epimedium All species of this plant are well worth a place on the rock garden. Their delicate foliage changes throughout the year from fresh green in spring to bronze in autumn. Unfortunately, the long sprays of flowers do not last long.

Geranium There are several low-growing geraniums that are fully hardy and therefore excellent for rock work. Perhaps the best is *G. dalmaticum* with its large pink flowers and dainty foliage.

Geum For really brilliant colouring, *G. coccineum* is not to be missed. Its bright orange flowers will compete with any other. Geums prefer a moist, semi-shaded situation.

Helleborous All the Christmas roses are worth considering, especially since they flower in late winter or very early spring. *H. niger* is the best known, but *H. macranthus,* the large-flowered form, is probably more striking. They all prefer a shaded position and a lime soil.

Helianthemum The rock roses are indispensable. They produce a profusion of flowers in many colours during June and July.

Hosta In damp spots, the hostas are a must. They are available in a variety of variegated foliage colours, and their show of flower makes them worthy of a place in any rockery.

Scabiosa A long succession of purple, pincushion flowers from June to September makes *S. graminifolia* well worth growing.

Veronica There are several non-shrubby veronicas that will provide a bright show of blue. *V. cinerea* is one of the best, making low-growing ash-grey mats of foliage with spikes of blue flower.

Helleborus niger

Shrubs and Conifers

Shrubs are often forgotten as suitable subjects for rock gardens, and yet they are among the least troublesome and easiest plants to cultivate.

Many ground-cover subjects are ideal in that they will cover space quickly and tumble over rocks, softening the hard lines. Other shrubs can be used as specimen plants to provide a focal point and to add height.

Make sure that you give them the sort of soil conditions they prefer. It is no good trying to grow most heathers, dwarf rhododendrons or azaleas, for example, in anything but an acid, peaty soil.

Acer palmatum and **A. japonica** types (bush form). These beautiful foliage plants need a sheltered situation to protect their delicate foliage. They can be obtained in delicate greens and deep crimsons, and their finely cut foliage is very attractive.

Berberis Many of the low-growing barberries make excellent rockery plants. *B. wilsonae, B. candidula* and *B. thunbergii* are particularly suitable. Some of these are evergreen, and have the added advantage of giving a show not only of flowers in the spring, but also of berries in the autumn.

Cotoneaster The large family of cotoneasters include some prostrate and semi-prostrate forms that will, like the barberries, follow their display of flowers with berries in abundance. *C. humifusus, C. microphyllus* and *C. salicifolius* 'Autumn Fire' are all worth their place.

Cytisus beanii is a charming dwarf shrub with golden yellow flowers in May, while *C. kewensis* sports masses of creamy coloured flowers at about the same time.

Euonymus 'Emerald 'n Gold' and *E.* 'Silver Queen' are trailing foliage plants whose names adequately describe their colouring.

Genista Two of the gorses are worth growing on the rockery. *G. hispanica,* the Spanish gorse, is especially good on a dry bank in a sunny position. It forms dense, prickly mounds covered in yellow flower. *G. lydia* has slender, pendulous branches and yellow flowers.

Hebe Many of the veronicas make good rockery subjects. Look out especially for *H. Carl Teschner, H. armstrongii* and *H. puingifolia* 'Pagei'.

Potentilla Another family of plants that thrive in the well-drained conditions of the rock garden. Most have masses of yellow or orange flowers, and the red-flowered *P.* 'Red Ace' is not to be missed.

Rhododendron and **Azalea** These aristocrats of the peat-lands can be obtained in dwarf form and are quite superb in spring. Make sure they are planted towards the top of the rock garden and that their planting pockets are filled with a peaty, acid soil.

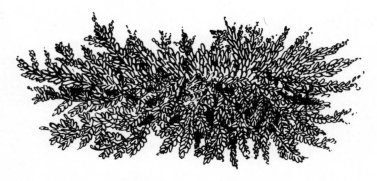

Juniperus communis depressa

Conifers Several dwarf and prostrate conifers will add a little height and set off the flowers of other plants. Make sure though, that the varieties you choose are truly dwarf or at least very slow-growing. Recommended are: *Chamaecyparis lawsoniana obtusa Nana Gracilis, C.l. Minima Aurea, C.l. obtusa Pygmea, C. pisifera plumosa Aurea Nana, Juniperus communis Depressa Aurea, J.c. Repanda, J. horizontalis Glauca, J.c. Compressa, Picea glauca Albertiana Conica, Thuya occidentalis Holmstrup, T.o. Rheingold, T. orientalis Aurea Nana.*

Illustrated by Barry Gurbutt

Hamilton, Geoff
Design and build a rockery.—
(Penny pinchers).
1. Rock gardens
I. Title   II. Series
712'.6   SB459
ISBN 0–7153–7901–1

Printed in Great Britain
by A. Wheaton & Co., Exeter
for David & Charles (Publishers) Limited
Brunel House   Newton Abbot   Devon

Published in the United States of America
by David & Charles Inc
North Pomfret   Vermont 05053   USA